The Saying

The Sayings Series

The Sayings of

HENRIK
IBSEN

edited by

Roland Huntford

DUCKWORTH

First published in 1996 by
Gerald Duckworth & Co. Ltd.
The Old Piano Factory
48 Hoxton Square, London N1 6PB
Tel: 0171 729 5986
Fax: 0171 729 0015

A catalogue record for this book is available
from the British Library

ISBN 0 7156 2668 X

Typeset by Ray Davies
Printed in Great Britain by
Redwood Books Ltd., Trowbridge

Contents

Sources

For an idea of how Ibsen appeared to his contemporaries, his *Collected Works* (Heinemann, 1906-08), the first such in English, is indispensable. In some ways it still captures the spirit of the original best of all. It is imbued with the fervour of the convert. The series was edited, and some of the plays translated, by William Archer.

The translation of *A Doll's House, The Wild Duck, The Lady from the Sea* (Everyman's Library, 1992) was originally published in 1910. Oddly enough, one of the translators was Eleanor Marx-Aveling, the youngest daughter of Karl Marx.

A good modern translation is *The Oxford Ibsen* (OUP, 1960-77). From this series comes *Four Major Plays* (The World's Classics, OUP, 1981).

The Cambridge Companion to Ibsen, by James McFarlane (CUP, 1994) is a useful introduction. For a marvellously informative browse there is George B. Bryan's encyclopaedic *An Ibsen Companion* (Greenwood Press, 1984). Amongst other things it lists all Ibsen's characters, and gives a stage history of his plays.

An accessible biography of Ibsen is Michael Meyer's compendious *Henrik Ibsen*, in three volumes (Rupert Hart-Davis, 1967-71); or abridged (Cardinal, 1992). For a vivid portrayal, Halvdan Koht's *The Life of Ibsen*, in two volumes (George Allen & Unwin, 1931), can hardly be bettered. It is a translation of a work by a formidable Norwegian scholar who wrote with verve. Edmund Gosse's *Ibsen* (Hodder and Stoughton, 1907) is essential historical reading. Together with William Archer, Sir Edmund Gosse accomplished the sisyphean task of introducing Ibsen to England.

Bernard Shaw's *The Quintessence of Ibsenism* (Constable, 1913) gives an insight into the effect of Ibsen on a contemporary playwright. It is also a notably Shavian illustration of how Ibsen could be misunderstood. Because Ibsen was a revolutionary, Shaw invoked him in support of his own brand of Socialism. But Ibsen, if anything, was a radical of the Right.

*

Except for some of the poetry, the translations in this book are the editor's own.

Introduction

Henrik Ibsen was one of the founders of modern drama.
His plays almost exactly span the second half of the
nineteenth century. During the last two decades, he was
a pioneering force in the theatre. He was a master of his
craft. He was an exemplar of the great man from a small
country; Norway in his case.

Ibsen was one of the surprising figures who emerged
from northern mists and helped to mould the age. They
were all products of the extraordinary Norwegian
renaissance of the nineteenth century. In music, for
example, there was Grieg; in exploration, Nansen, the
founder of modern polar travel, and Amundsen, the
conqueror of the South Pole; in art, Edvard Munch, the
Expressionist painter; in literature, Knut Hamsun, a
pioneer of the stream of consciousness and the
existentialist novel, and in mathematics, the
revolutionary genius of Nils Henrik Abel. There were
others too. All this is not bad for a poor country of two
million inhabitants at the time, on the periphery of
Europe. The forces of nationalism had a hand in events.
Norway was then subject to Sweden, but had begun the
long march to independence. This finally came in 1905
without, incidentally, a drop of blood being spilled.

Ibsen was born on 10 March 1828 at Skien, in the
province of Telemark, in southern Norway. His father's
business failed when Henrik was still a small boy.
Money was chronically short, as a result of which when
Ibsen was fifteen, his schooling had to stop. He left home
more or less destitute, and in 1844 was apprenticed to a
pharmacist in Grimstad, a sleepy little port on the south
coast of Norway. For the next six years, there he stayed.

On the face of it, this was not exactly a propitious
background. Ibsen's childhood, however, was passed in
a poor but cultivated milieu. His mother had a taste for
literature and drama which, in Ibsen himself, became a
passion. In Grimstad he began writing poetry. There, in

1849, at the age of 21, he finished his first play, *Catiline*, in blank verse. The eponymous Roman hero was significantly an aristocratic rebel.

In 1850 Ibsen moved to Christiania, as Oslo, the Norwegian capital, was then called. In the same year, his second play, *The Burial Mound*, another historical drama, was produced in a Christiania theatre – the first of his works to be performed. In 1852 he was appointed director and resident playwright at a newly established theatre in Bergen, the second city of Norway. He was obliged by contract to write a play a year; which religiously he did. After six years, now married, he returned to Christiania as a theatre manager.

In the meantime Ibsen had begun to suffer from the tragic sense of being trapped that is the shadow side of life in a small country. He longed for the world outside. Finally, supported by a modest state grant and private charity, he found the money to escape. In 1864 he went to Italy, not to return to live in Norway for 27 years.

The result was an object lesson in the influence of surroundings on the artist. Hitherto, Ibsen had shown conventional promise. He was known only in Norway. Now he settled in Rome, and over the next three years, in a state of intellectual intoxication – 'with vine leaves in his hair', to use his own phrase – wrote his great verse-dramas, *Brand* and *Peer Gynt*. They were paeans to individuality, and both instant literary sensations. They led to Ibsen's first breakthrough. He was now established in his own country, but his success spilled over into the rest of Scandinavia.

In 1868 Ibsen moved to Germany which, under Bismarck, for all its faults, he found full of energy and perversely stimulating. He lived there for the next ten years, first in Dresden, later in Munich. By now, besides being a dramatist, Ibsen was an acknowledged Norwegian poet, but in Germany he came to the conclusion that poetry was obsolescent. He deliberately abandoned it and, in his own words, turned to the 'incomparably more difficult art of writing purely realistic everyday language'.

One outcome was surprisingly *Emperor and Galilean*,

set in fourth-century Constantinople, about the ambiguous figure of Julian the Apostate. Ibsen perversely considered this to be his best play. It certainly cost him most effort. It provides some memorable sayings, but has rarely been performed. *Emperor and Galilean* was a painful act of metamorphosis. It neatly divides Ibsen's production chronologically into two coherent groups of twelve plays each. It marked his abandonment of verse, and his farewell to romantic, indeed gothic historical drama, which had so far been his stock in trade, in favour of the present. It was also his transition to the drama of ideas. It set his intellectual course. The culmination of all this was *Pillars of Society*, his next play, his first mature 'modern' work, and the forerunner of what was to come. Its message is encapsulated in the last line: 'The spirit of truth and freedom – *those* are the pillars of society.' The play was produced in Berlin in January 1878, and Ibsen thereby established his reputation in Germany.

Meanwhile, in 1878 Ibsen returned to live in Rome. There (and at Amalfi) he wrote *A Doll's House*, and with it, at the age of 51, finally burst out into the wider world. The first performance of the play took place in Copenhagen on 21 September 1879. The following spring saw first German productions in Munich and Berlin.

A Doll's House was the first of what are now recognised as Ibsen's great social and psychological plays to make a universal impact. In a cloud of shock, controversy and scandal, it quickly spread from Germany across the civilized world. It was a sensation. It divided the thinking classes into bitterly hostile camps of Ibsenites and their opponents.

The theme of the play was highly inflammatory. It deals with the break-up of a marriage, which was not exactly revolutionary, but the treatment was. Ibsen portrayed the marriage of Nora and Torvald Helmer, the protagonists of the play, as breaking up not because of a grand passion, which would have followed convention, but as a result of inherent dishonesty and strain, which very definitely did not. What is more, Ibsen suggested that Nora was justified in trying to find herself and putting duty to herself above her obligations to her husband and children.

But it was the technique of *A Doll's House* that was truly disturbing. Ibsen had achieved his aim of a realistic drama with realistic dialogue. That was the heart of the Ibsen revolution. Thus he overturned reigning concepts and founded the modern theatre. He showed that ordinary middle-class people in ordinary middle-class situations could be convincingly put on stage. By stripping uncomfortable issues of heroics and romance, he brought them home to his audience. In that sense, today, our drama is all Ibsenesque.

After *A Doll's House*, there followed regularly every other year or so the plays that made Ibsen's name and have endured: *Ghosts*, which caused a furore by breaking several taboos in dealing with venereal disease, incest and mercy killing; *An Enemy of the People*, *The Wild Duck*, and *Rosmersholm*. In 1885 Ibsen moved back to Germany, to Munich, where he wrote *Hedda Gabler*, whose heroine is arguably one of the great female rôles in Western drama. *The Master Builder*, about the conflict between youth and age, was written after he returned to live in Norway in 1891. There were other plays, but these constitute what might be called the Ibsen canon. Ibsen's last play, *When We Dead Awaken*, appeared in 1899. He died in Christiania in 1906.

From *The Wild Duck* onwards, Ibsen's plays were translated and performed abroad as soon as they were written. Of no other contemporary dramatist can that be said. It needs a touch of the Titan to escape from the bounds of a small language. Ibsen changed the theatre in the Western world. He is as much a part of the drama in England, America and Germany as in his native land.

But Ibsen is not merely a formative figure from the past. He remains compulsive reading in his own right. Like the ancient Greek dramatists, he possessed the magical ability to turn squabbling local characters – his essential plays are all set in Norway – into universal figures. Again like the Greeks, at the very opening of his plays he has the mysterious gift of somehow contriving to convey an undercurrent of something awry.

However, unlike even the Greeks, or Shakespeare for that matter, Ibsen questioned the fundamentals of his society. He also caught the spirit of the times while it was still germinating. This is a rare and lethal talent. The sum of it all has been to make Ibsen a profoundly disturbing and ambiguous figure.

Like the ancient Greek dramatists, and for much the same reason, Ibsen is torture to translate. The nineteenth-century Norwegian in which he wrote was a very fine literary language. But like Greek it has a mythic content which English does not possess. In translation what remains are plot, character and action. Whole levels of meaning are left behind. This is a pity, for in his native Norwegian, Ibsen is a master of language. He played upon the sub-text. Like many great dramatists, he helped to form his own tongue.

Ibsen, again like the Greeks, works and reworks a few constant themes. His great underlying motif is the power of the past. Both in his life and his work, he was trying to cast it off. From his early plays, his hallmark was something from the past emerging to haunt the present. Always in his later, famous plays he is concerned with the conflict of new ideas with the old.

Individuality is the other great Ibsen theme. From this comes the need for the realization of the self, a hatred of compromise; a love of the individual, a loathing of the collective, and the conflict between the two – this last exemplified by *An Enemy of the People*.

On various occasions, Ibsen somewhat disingenuously disclaimed responsibility for the opinions of his characters. What he really meant was that he hid behind them. He had a proper horror of being didactic on the stage. He had the peculiar genius of avoiding puppetry, and making his characters appear to be thinking for themselves, so that he himself was invisible.

Ibsen was not a voluminous correspondent nor, by his own admission, a willing one. Nonetheless, when the spirit moved, he could be trenchant and inspired. For this, he needed anger – his operating mode. One of his most entertaining aspects was his fury with his fellow-countrymen. In his attachment to landscape, a sense of being bewitched by the sea, a penchant for self-criticism, and a gift for polemic, Ibsen was thoroughly Norwegian. In all his writings, however, it is difficult to find a word of praise for his fellow-countrymen. *Peer Gynt* is partly a disdainful exposé of what Ibsen saw as Norwegian failings – notably parochialism and shrinking before great events.

Although Ibsen unquestionably concentrated on the shadow side, he had considerable wit and much wry humour, as these sayings reveal. It is a mistake to say that he wrote tragedies; they were black comedies. In an age falling into demotic tyranny, he was an exponent of aristocratic radicalism. He had a profound mistrust of the whole tribe of politicians. He once wrote of the 'ship called Europe' sailing 'with a corpse on board!' After more than a century, Ibsen remains a man for the millennium.

Politics

Today the ideal of leadership,
Turns out to be a corporal.   *Brand*, Act V, 1866

... The State
Loathes freedom like the very plague,
But loves equality all too well.   *ibid.*

Krogstad: The law does not ask about motives.
Nora: Then the law must be very bad.
                                   A Doll's House, Act I, 1879

The worship of authority *must* be exterminated.
                         An Enemy of the People, Act II, 1882

I know the local authorities so well; those in power do not
willingly accept proposals emanating from others.   *ibid.*

Dr Stockmann: But how on earth do you really propose to
    demonstrate?
Aslaksen: With great moderation, naturally, Herr Doktor; I
    always deal in moderation, for moderation, you see, is the
    greatest virtue of a citizen.   *ibid.*

The public is best served by the good old accepted thoughts it
already has.   *ibid.*

The damned, compact, liberal majority.   *ibid.*, Act IV

That the ordinary man, the masses, the crowd are the true heart
of the people [is] just a newspaper lie, you see! The crowd is
nothing but the raw material out of which the people will make
people.   *ibid.*

A normally constructed truth lasts – as a rule, if I may say so –
for 17-18 years; 20 at the most; rarely longer. But such senile
truths are always horribly emaciated. Nonetheless it is only
then that the majority accepts them, and recommends them to
society as true intellectual fodder. But there is not much
nourishment in that kind of diet, I can assure you.   *ibid.*

To begin with, I will keep to *one* approved truth which is fundamentally a horrible lie … that belief that the ordinary people, the crowd, the common herd, are the heart of the nation – that they are the nation itself.   *ibid.*

That kind of herd that I am speaking of, is not only found in the lower depths; it seethes and swarms around us, right up to the top of society. Just look at … my brother … your own glorious, respectable magistrate! [He] is just as good a man of the common herd as any that stand on two feet … not because he, like me, is descended from a foul old pirate from Pomerania or thereabouts … but because he thinks the thoughts of his superiors, and because he mouths the opinions of his superiors.   *ibid.*

Open-mindedness is virtually the same as morality.

ibid.

I am so fond of the town in which I was born that I would rather destroy it than see it flourish because of a lie.

ibid.

I am thinking of those few among us who have absorbed all the young, germinating truths. These men are, as it were, out among the pioneers, so far ahead that the compact majority has not reached that point – and *there* they fight for the truths which are still too fresh in the world of consciousness to have any majority supporting them.   *ibid.*

The majority has *power* – unfortunately – but it is not *right*. It is the few others and I, the individuals, who are right.

ibid.

Who make up the majority of the inhabitants of a country? Are they the sensible people or the stupid ones? I think that we agree that stupid people are present in a frighteningly overwhelming majority right round the whole wide world. But God help me, it cannot be right that the stupid shall rule over the intelligent for the whole of eternity.   *ibid.*

The masses, the majority, this damned, compact majority [are] what poison our spiritual sources and pollute the earth underfoot.   *ibid.*

The minority is always right.   *ibid.*

The most dangerous enemies of truth and freedom among us are the compact majority.

ibid.

The worst of it is that all people are party serfs.

ibid., Act V

The craziest of all is that adult liberal people wander around in masses and delude both themselves and others that they are liberal-minded!

ibid.

It is the party leaders who must be exterminated.

ibid.

The liberals are the most sinister enemies of free men.

ibid.

Party manifestos wring the necks of all young, living truths.

ibid.

Considerations of expediency turn morality and justice upside down, so that in the end it becomes quite horrible.

ibid.

One should never put on one's best trousers when one goes out to fight for liberty and truth.

ibid.

The strongest man in the world is he who is most alone.

ibid.

Oh, all this about law and order! Sometimes I think *that* is what causes all unhappiness in the world.

Ghosts, Act II, 1881

Pastor Manders: Is there not a little voice in your mother's heart that stops you breaking down your son's ideals?
Mrs Alving: But what about the truth?

ibid.

It is the great public that has to support a newspaper; but the great public is the bad public – that follows from the nature of local politics; and a bad public wants a bad newspaper. So that, you see, is how I edited the newspaper.

The League of Youth, Act II, 1869

Being stupid, the Devil was in a plight,
His audience he did not judge aright.

Peer Gynt, Act V

Consul Bernick: I have also learned this during the last few days: it is you women who are the pillars of society.
Miss Hessel: Then you have learned a shaky lesson ... Oh no; the spirit of truth and freedom – *those* are the pillars of society.

Pillars of Society, Act IV, 1877

Relling: He is suffering from acute righteousness fever.
Gina: Righteousness fever?
Hedvig: Is that a disease?
Relling: Oh yes; it's a national disease, but it only breaks out sporadically.   *The Wild Duck*, Act III, 1884

Don't use the foreign word: ideals. We have a good native word: lies.   *ibid.*, Act V

Your seed is sprouting. How fiery the heat!
You're confused; you know neither whither nor why –
For stilettos are growing instead of the wheat!

'The Murder of Abraham Lincoln', 1871

[Of politicians]: These pocket-sized souls.

Letter, 1865

Now they have taken Rome away from us human beings and given it to the politicians.   Letter, 1870

For every statesman that appears ... an artist is destroyed.

ibid.

Is it not villainous of the 'Commune' in Paris to have spoiled my excellent theory of the state, or rather theory of the non-state! Now the idea is destroyed for a long time, and I cannot even decently present it in verse.   Letter, 1871

The situation ... is not so much the fruit of any particularly
brilliant gifts on the part of the leaders of the opposition, but
much more the result of utterly indefensible cowardice,
capitulation and compromise among nearly all those whose
duty it ought to be to defend the foundations of our society.

Letter, 1872

Liberals ... are poor creatures with whom to man the
barricades.   Letter, 1882

And what is one to say of the circumstances of the so-called
liberal press? Those leaders who talk and write about liberty
and broad-mindedness, and who in consequence
simultaneously turn themselves into the slaves of the supposed
opinions of their subscribers!

ibid.

There is something demoralising in busying oneself with
politics and joining parties.

ibid.

And what about all these much-vaunted advocates of freedom?
Is the work of liberation only to be allowed in the field of
politics? ... Is it not above all the spirit that needs liberation?
Serfs' souls like ours cannot even enjoy the freedoms we
already have.   *ibid.*

I have learned to know the peasants in many countries, but
nowhere have I found them to be liberal, self-sacrificing or
altruistic; on the contrary, everywhere I have found that they
cling to the uttermost degree to their rights and their own
advantage.

Letter, 1883

I am also a heathen in the political field, I do not believe in the
liberating power of politics, nor do I believe much in the
unselfishness or goodwill of those in power.

ibid.

The Human Condition

Whatever you are, it must be out and out,
Not tepid, divided or in doubt.   *Brand*, Act I, 1866

Help is useless for a man,
Who doesn't want what he cannot do.   *ibid.*

Room within the world's wide span,
Self completely to fulfil.
That's a valid right of Man,
And no more than that I will.   *ibid.*, Act II

His faults, his virtues do not go far,
He is a dwarf in big and small,
A dwarf in evil, a dwarf in good.   *ibid.*

Willpower is what really counts,
Willpower liberates or shatters.   *ibid.*, Act II

Being unable, you can be forgiven,
But never if you lack the will.   *ibid.*, Act III

Only what is lost is kept for ever.   *ibid.*, Act IV

If by fighting you cannot win,
With gentleness you must advance.   *ibid.*

A man is fashioned for his work,
His goal is paradise for him.   *ibid.*

All roads are equally good,
As long as they lead to the goal.   *ibid.*, Act V

A promise is a future pact,
In the future it will be kept.   *ibid.*

To *promise* is in the end to *lie*.   *ibid.*

Mrs Linde: But really, my dear Nora – haven't you acted rashly?
Nora: Is it rash to save your husband's life?

A Doll's House, Act I, 1879

Rank: I don't know if in your part of the country you also have
   a kind of person that bustles around panting in order to
   sniff out moral corruption and then have those in question
   put in for observation in some suitable post. The healthy
   people just have to accept that they remain outside.
Mrs Linde: But it is surely the invalids who most need to be
   locked up.
Rank: Exactly. There you are. It is that point of view that turns
   society into a hospital.   *ibid.*

No one knows what bad people can contrive.   *ibid.*, Act II

He is an acquaintance of my youth. It is one of those hasty
acquaintances that are so often an embarrassment later in life.
ibid.

Life has taught me not to believe in well turned phrases.
ibid., Act III

I should like to mention dogs, to which we human beings are
so closely related.   *An Enemy of the People*, Act IV, 1882

A cruel word can be like the scratch of a pin in the lungs.
ibid., Act V

Into isolation? Really? In isolation one broods. I forbid you to
brood.

Emperor and Galilean, Part I, Act I, 1873

Wine is the soul of the grape.   *ibid.*, Act III

It is the true spirit of rebellion to demand happiness in life.
Ghosts, Act I, 1881

He was that kind of person whose way of life does not affect
his reputation.   *ibid.*

There, you see the power of a bad conscience.   *ibid.*

Mother, give me the sun.   *ibid.*, Act III

I see him before me. With vine leaves in his hair.

Hedda Gabler, Act II, 1890

And now – the great thing, which has such beauty in it. That he had the strength and willpower to break up from the banquet of life – so soon. *ibid.*

Tesman: She has shot herself! Shot herself in the temple! Think of that!
Brack: God have mercy on us – that's simply *not done*!

ibid., Act IV

I feel like a Napoleon who has been crippled in his first battle.

John Gabriel Borkman, Act II, 1896

No one argues on top of a meal; it doesn't do any good.

The League of Youth, Act II, 1869

Forged young man; forged; as clear as my name is Daniel. One only needs to look at it with the sharpened gaze of mistrust.

ibid., Act IV

Perhaps I'll even run my ship aground,
Still it is lovely to sail!

Love's Comedy, Act I, 1862

Through life there is a Nemesis that runs,
With certainty it finds its mark, though late,
To no one is it given to escape. *ibid.*, Act III

A home is where there is plenty of room for five,
Although among enemies it seems cramped for two.

ibid.

Now you can choose in freedom. And on your own responsibility.

The Lady from the Sea, Act V, 1888

Once and for all I *am* what I *am*. Nor can I create myself anew.

The Master Builder, Act I, 1892

Ah well, after a good dinner, one doesn't care about the pennies.

ibid.

Solness: No. I don't build any more church towers any longer.
    Nor any churches either.
Hilde: Well then, what are you building *now*?
Solness: Homes for people.   *ibid.*

Have you never noticed that the impossible seems to entice and
call?

                                                    ibid., Act II

Sometimes I wonder if you haven't been born into the world
with a sickly conscience.

                                                    ibid.

In a way he *is* afraid. He, the great master builder. He's not
afraid to take the joy of life from other people – as he has done
with my father and myself. But just to climb up on a miserable
scaffolding – *that* he will pray God to preserve him from!

                                                    ibid., Act III

Solness: The only thing I believe can contain human happiness
    – *that* is what I want to build now.
Hilde: Master builder – now you mean our castles in the air.
Solness: Yes, castles in the air.

                                                    ibid.

A lie can be turned upside down,
Decorated with much show,
Dressed up in a whole new self,
Its carcass quite unrecognised.   *Peer Gynt*, Act I, 1867

If I beat or I am beaten,
There'll be wailing just the same.   *ibid.*

You have to trust in the power of habit.

                                                    ibid., Act II

You won't fish me with lies as bait!   *ibid.*

Back and forth, it is just as far;
In or out, it is just as cramped.   *ibid.*

Peer Gynt: Answer me! Who are you?
A voice in the darkness: Myself!
Peer Gynt: Out of the way!
The voice: Go roundabout Peer! There is plenty of space.
Peer Gynt (tries to pass elsewhere, but is stopped): Who are *you*?
The voice: Myself. Can you say the same? …
Peer Gynt: *What are* you?
The voice: The Great Crooked One.

ibid.

To think of it, wish it, even to have the will –
But to *do* it! No, that I do not understand.

ibid., Act III

I have always tried to be myself.

ibid., Act IV

It's a bad business, being a prophet!

ibid.

Having a soul a man is bound,
  By looking inward on the self.

ibid.

The essence of the art of daring,
The art of bravery in deed,
Is this, to move with nimble foot,
Through the cunning snares of life,
To recognise that other days
Remain beyond the day of battle,
To know that ever in the rear,
Stands a bridge for your retreat.
This is the theory that has borne me on,
All my conduct it has coloured;
And this same theory I inherit,
From my flesh and blood in my childhood home.

ibid.

Who nothing owns will lightly dare.
When in the world one scarce commands
The strip of earth one's shadow shields,
For cannon fodder you are made.

ibid.

Let the Lord rule ...
Only trust in him, He knows how much
Of the chalice of need I can bear to drink.
He takes a fatherly interest in my wellbeing –
But an economist – Oh no, he is not!

ibid.

Golden stirrups to hold my feet!
Great men you may know by their riding gear!

ibid.

To be yourself on grounds of gold,
Is like building your house on shifting sands.

ibid.

There is a text or else a saying,
Somewhere, I don't remember where,
That if you gained the whole wide world,
But lost yourself, your gain were but
A garland on a cloven crown.

ibid.

I'd better follow them on their way,
While protesting loudly to high Heaven.

ibid.

Peer Gynt: At worst you may call me a bungler of sorts,
But really not an exceptional sinner.
The Button Founder: But *that* is just the rub, my man.
In a higher sense, you're no sinner at all.
That's why you're excused the pangs of purgatory,
To land like others in the casting ladle.

ibid., Act V

Strength and determination are needed for a sin.

ibid.

Round about said the Crooked One! No this time,
Straight through, be the path never so cramped.

ibid.

That wretch can fly
So fast, as fast as Peer Gynt can lie.

ibid.

Peer Gynt: The old crystal-gazer's joke,
No emperor thou, but an onion instead.
Well now I will peel you my dear old Peer ...
(*Takes an onion and peels layer after layer.*)
... What an unbearable number of skins!
Is the kernel not soon about to appear?
My God it does not! To the heart of hearts,
It is all layers, only smaller and smaller –
Nature is witty!   *ibid.*

Now you're safe; be happy too – if you can.
                                    Pillars of Society, Act IV, 1877

A man can die for another man's ambition, But if he wants to
stay alive, he must live for his own.
                                    The Pretenders, Act IV, 1864

I rule over a hundred wise heads, a thousand ready arms, but
not over *one* loving, trusty heart. That *is* royal destitution.
                                    ibid.

King Skule: I *must* have someone by my side who obeys me
    without a will of his own – who believes unbendingly in
    me, who will stand by me through thick and thin, who lives
    only to cast light and warmth over my life, who will die
    with me if I fall. Tell me what to do ...
Jatgeir: Buy a dog, my lord.   *ibid.*

Skule Bårdsson was God's stepchild on earth; *that* was his
enigma.   *ibid.*, Act V

Kroll: Good Lord – so *that* was the Ulrik Brendel whom people
    once believed would make his mark.
Rosmer: At any rate, he has had the courage to live according to
    his own ideas. I don't think *that's* too bad.
                                    Rosmersholm, Act I, 1886

Rebecca: Rosmer likes to have fresh, live flowers around him.
Kroll: I think you do so too.
Rebecca: Yes. I think they numb the senses so nicely.
                                    ibid.

[He] is able to live without ideals. And *that* you see, *that* is the
great secret of action and victory. That's the sum and substance
of all the world's wisdom. Nothing more!   *ibid.*, Act IV

Put an eagle in a cage, and it will bite the bars, whether they be of iron or gold.

The Vikings at Helgeland, Act II, 1858

A lonely man does not laugh so easily.

The Wild Duck, Act I, 1884

It is good for the digestion to sit and look at pictures.

ibid.

If I am unreasonable now and then – good God – remember that I am stormed by an army of sorrows … No beer at a moment such as this. Give me my flute. *ibid.*, Act II

Relling: Almost everyone is sick, unfortunately.
Gregers: And what cure are you using for Hjalmar?
Relling: My usual one. I take care to preserve the life-lie in him.
Gregers: The life-lie? I don't think I heard correctly –
Relling: Oh yes, I said the life-lie. For the life-lie, you see, is the
   stimulating force. *ibid.*, Act V

If you take the life-lie from an average person, you take away his happiness immediately. *ibid.*

Ah well, life could be quite pleasant just the same, if only we could be free of these blessed creditors who pester us poor people with their idealistic demands. *ibid.*

In my view, to fulfil oneself through one's way of life is the highest that a human being can attain. Each one of us has that goal, but most of us betray it.

Letter, 1882

Rosmersholm … deals with the struggle that every thinking person has to pursue with himself in order to bring his way of life into harmony with his perception.

Letter, 1887

The various intellectual faculties do not develop evenly and equally in one and the same person. The acquisitive instinct forges ahead from profit to profit. Moral consciousness, on the other hand, 'Conscience', is extremely retrogressive. It has deep roots in tradition and the past in general. From that the conflict within the individual stems.

ibid.

Women & Marriage

Mrs Linde: Since then, have you never confided in your
husband?
Nora: No, for Heaven's sake, how can you imagine such a
thing? ... Torvald with his manly pride – how painful and
humiliating it would be for him to know that he owed me
anything. It would quite disturb the relations between us;
our beautiful, happy home would no longer be what it is.

A Doll's House, Act I, 1879

My little Nora, there is a considerable difference between your
father and myself. Your father was no impeccable
office-holder. But that is what I am.

ibid., Act II

To work for oneself is no pleasure ... find me someone and
something to work for.

ibid., Act III

You have never loved me. You have only thought it was
enjoyable to be in love with me.

ibid.

Nora: When I was at home with my father, he told me all his
opinions, and then I had the same opinions, and if I had
others, I hid them; for he would not have liked it. He called
me his doll-child, and he played with me as I played with
my dolls. And then I came into your house.
Helmer: What kind of things are you saying about our
marriage?
Nora: I mean that I went straight from papa's hands into yours.

ibid.

You aren't the man to bring me up to be the right wife for you.

ibid.

Helmer: No one sacrifices his *honour* for the one he loves.
Nora: A hundred thousand women have done so.

ibid.

Helmer: Have you never been happy here?
Nora: No, never. I believed I was, but I have never been so.
Helmer: Not – not happy!
Nora: No; only merry.   *ibid.*

Helmer: This is outrageous. You will fail your most sacred duty.
Nora: What do you call my most sacred duty?
Helmer As if I needed to tell you! Is it not your duty towards
    your husband and your children?
Nora: I have another duty just as sacred.
Helmer: You do not. Which duty to you mean?
Nora: Duty to myself.   *ibid.*

Helmer: First and foremost you are a wife and mother.
Nora: I don't believe that any more. I believe that I am first and
    foremost a human being.   *ibid.*

I can no longer be satisfied with what most people say, and
what is found in books. I will have to think things over myself,
and try to understand them.   *ibid.*

Just as before, I was your little song bird, your doll, whom now
you would have to handle with extra care, since it was so
brittle and frail [and] at that moment I realised that I had lived
with a strange man for eight years, and that I had three
children – I can't bear to think of it! I could tear myself to
shreds.   *ibid.*

Helmer: Nora, – Can I never be more than a stranger to you?
Nora: Ah no, Torvald, in that case the wonder of wonders must
    happen.
Helmer: Name this wonder of wonders!
Nora: That you and I change so that – Ah Torvald, I don't
    believe in wonders any longer.
Helmer: But I will believe. Name it! Change ourselves so that – ?
Nora: That the life we share might become a marriage. Farewell.
                                              ibid., Act III

A wife is not supposed to be her husband's judge
                                              Ghosts, Act I, 1881

Pastor Manders: My head is almost going round. Your
    marriage – all your life of many years together with your
    husband was nothing more than a concealed abyss!
Mrs Alving: Not a whit more. Now you know.   *ibid.*

Ah, the joy of life, mother, you don't know much about it in this home.   *ibid.*, Act II

We male creatures must not judge a poor woman too harshly.
                                                                    ibid.

You have failed the women you *loved!* Me, me, me! The most precious thing you have in the whole world, you were prepared to give up for the sake of profit. *That* is the double murder you have committed! The murder of your own soul, and mine.
                                        John Gabriel Borkman, Act II, 1896

The great, unforgivable sin, is the sin of murdering the love-life within a person.   *ibid.*

Ellida! ... You think and feel in images – and in visible ideas.
                                        The Lady from the Sea, Act V, 1888

If one marries into an uneducated family, in a way one marries the whole family.

                                        The League of Youth, Act II, 1869

He was rough, and he drank as well; but a man is a man all the same.   *ibid.*, Act IV

But my dear Rita, the human metamorphosis down the years; at some time it must happen in *our* life together. Exactly like everyone else.

                                                Little Eyolf, Act I, 1894

Ah, my dear Rita, it is no use demanding anything. Everything must be given voluntarily.

                                                                    ibid.

When happiness finally comes, it usually comes like a spring flood.   *ibid.*

Solness: I have never sung a note in my life.
Hilde: Oh yes, you sang that time. It sounded like harps in the air.

                                        The Master Builder, Act I, 1892

He was too strong. Women stood behind him.

                                                Peer Gynt, Act II, 1867

Possessed of a woman, I was a silver-clasped book,
It's the same printing error to be mad or sane!

ibid., Act IV

To love, sacrifice everything and be forgotten; that is my saga.

The Pretenders, Act IV, 1864

Nobody knows what a woman is capable of!

The Vikings at Helgeland, Act II, 1858

Relling: A *child* also belongs to a marriage. And you must leave
the child alone.
Hjalmar: Ah Hedvig! My poor little Hedvig!
Relling: Exactly, you must keep Hedvig out of it. You two are
grown up people; for God's sake, you may bungle your
relationship if you wish to. But be careful with Hedvig, I
say; otherwise you do her an injury … or she can do an
injury to herself – and perhaps others too.

The Wild Duck, Act IV, 1884

It was only when I was married that my life acquired
significant content.

Letter, 1870

[My wife] is is exactly the character I need – illogical, but with a
strong poetic instinct, with great broad-mindedness, and an
almost violent hatred of all meanness.

ibid.

It is women who will solve the human predicament.

Speech to the Norwegian Feminist Union, 1898

Precisely because [Mrs. Alving in *Ghosts*] is a woman, she will
go to the uttermost extremes when once she has begun.

Letter, 1882

The Arts & the Intellect

Ideas slake no one's thirst,
Ideas do not hunger sate   *Brand*, Act IV, 1866

Compromise, thy name is Satan!   *ibid.*, Act V

A little finger was demanded,
In order to take the whole hand of mine!
Look there is the spirit of compromise!   *ibid.*

The classroom is a fencing gymnasium for thought and talent.
                    Emperor and Galilean, Part I, Act I, 1873

Look at that royal Galilean; he is an intellectual Achilles.
                    ibid.

You Galileans have made truth an exile.   *ibid.*

Prince Julian: While I lead this life of storm and uproar, I
    sometimes think that truth is the enemy of beauty.
Basilius from Caesarea: And at such a moment can you sigh for
    beauty?   *ibid.*, Act II

The same answer in desperation. Books – always books! …
Stones for bread … I can't use books; – it is life I hunger for.
                    ibid.

The old beauty is no longer beautiful and the new truth is no
longer true.
                    ibid.

Maximus the Mystic: There are three kingdoms … First is that
    kingdom founded on the tree of knowledge, and then that
    kingdom founded on the wood of the Cross.
Prince Julian: And the third?
Maximus the Mystic: The third is the kingdom … that will be
    founded on the tree of knowledge and the wood of the
    Cross, because it loves and hates both and because it has its
    living sources under Adam's garden and under Golgotha.
                    ibid., Act III

Don't leave out any of the exclamation marks! Rather add a
few!   *An Enemy of the People*, Act III, 1882

Allmers: I had a feeling that I was really misusing or – no,
    neglecting by best qualities. That I was squandering my
    time.
Asta: When you were sitting and writing your book?
Allmers (*nodding*): Because surely I do not only have the ability
    for *that* alone. I must be able to accomplish something else
    as well.   *Little Eyolf*, Act I, 1894

Thinking; ah *that* conveys the best in oneself. What appears on
paper is not worth much.   *ibid.*

You simply gave your Muse a kick,
And she set to work.   *Love's Comedy*, Act I, 1862

It seems as if the desire to write is contagious.   *ibid.*

How dare you accuse me of writing verse.   *ibid.*, Act II

Is the world not everywhere the same,
And on every man's wall is there not,
The same lie in truth's glass and frame?   *ibid.*, Act III

The riddle was once black; now it seems grey.
                                    Peer Gynt, Act II, 1867

Faith goes unhindered; it is duty free.   *ibid.*

If we agree on food and clothes,
You may certainly call faith what we call fear.   *ibid.*

I have forgotten what I never have known.
                                               ibid., Act III

Shrewdness, taken to extremes, is folly.
                                               ibid., Act IV

You must not read to swallow words,
But to see what you can use.   *ibid.*

When the point of departure is maddest of all,
The result is often the most original.   *ibid.*

In truth a highly gifted man,
Almost all he utters, goes over my head.   *ibid.*

Don't worry; you'll survive
No one dies in the middle of Act Five.   *ibid.*, Act V

A false assumption, which has now been left behind.   *ibid.*

Finally he stood revealed,
He was a dismal moralist.   *ibid.*

Horrible people, these scientists!   *ibid.*

Jatgeir: I received the gift of sorrow, and so I became a poet.
King Skule: So the gift of sorrow is what the poet needs?
Jatgeir: I needed sorrow; there may be others who need faith or
    happiness – or doubt.   *The Pretenders*, Act IV, 1864

King Skule: Do you have many unwritten poems?
Jatgeir: No, but many unborn ones; they are conceived one by
    one, acquire life, and then they are born.   *ibid.*

Unwritten poems are always the most beautiful.   *ibid.*

In every work of poetry there must be a few lies.   *ibid.*

No poem is born in daylight; it can be written down in
sunlight, but it is created in the silent watches of the night.
                    ibid.

From the infernal regions I come ...
And in order a suitable stage to attain,
In fact down there just to get in,
It is strictly required to have learned Latin.

                    ibid., Act V

The mysterious satisfaction of creating.
                    Rosmersholm, Act I, 1886

Brendel: My most significant works are known to neither man
    nor woman. To no one – except myself.
Rebecca: How can *that* be?
Brendel: Because they have not been written.

                    ibid.

This dismal craft of writing has always aroused in me a
suffocating distaste. *ibid.*

I live so quickly, Maja. That is the way we artists live.
When We Dead Awaken, Act II, 1899

The poet within him was too strong!
'Without a Name', 1872

Do you remember 'The Tragic Muse' that stands in the …
Vatican? No piece of sculpture down here has carried so much
explanation as this one. I dare maintain that it is through this
that it has been borne on me what Greek tragedy was. That
indescribably great, lofty and calm happiness in the expression
of the face, the rich head, crowned with a laurel wreath, that
has something supernaturally devouring and Bacchanalian;
eyes that at the same time look inwards to themselves and also
right through and beyond those that are looking on – such was
Greek tragedy. Letter, 1867

There is nothing stable in the world of ideas.
Letter, 1867

Talent is no privilege, it is a duty. *ibid.*

The State has its roots in time; with time, it will come to an end.
Greater things will fall; all religion will fall. Neither moral
concepts nor art forms have any touch of eternity. How much
are we really obliged to cling to? Who will assure me that 2 and
2 are not five up on Jupiter? Letter, 1871

The business of a poet is fundamentally to *see*, not to analyse;
in my case, I would see danger there. *ibid.*

The liberals are the worst enemies of freedom. Freedom of
thought and spiritual freedom grow best under absolutism;
that has been demonstrated in France, later in Germany, and
now in Russia. Letter, 1872

I am convinced that in half the time that you must have taken
for the translation [of John Stuart Mill], you could have written
a book that was ten times better yourself. I also think that you
are doing Stuart Mill a grave injustice in doubting the truth of
his assurance that he has acquired all his ideas from his wife.
Letter, 1873

The deterioration in the power of judgment that is a necessary consequence of an extensive pursuit of theological studies, at least in the case of the average person, is particularly evident when it is a question of judging human character, human actions, and human motives.   Letter, 1882

This actor's appearance does not really suit a man who cannot bear the thought of warm food for supper, who has a weak stomach, a bad digestion and who lives on weak tea.
> Letter to the director of a Christiania theatre on the
> first production of *An Enemy of the People*, 1882

In the so-called romantic drama … illusion is not an absolute requirement; during a performance every spectator is perfectly aware that he is only sitting in a theatre and watching a theatrical performance.

But circumstances will be different when *An Enemy of the People* is produced. Each member of the audience must feel as if he were invisibly present in Dr Stockmann's living room; everything must be realistic here.   *ibid.*

I have now finished the draft of my new work, a play in 5 acts [*The Wild Duck*], and am heavily engaged in revision; the fine polishing of the language and a more pronounced invidualising of characters and dialogue.   Letter, 1883

An intellectual order of ability cannot easily be reconciled with democratic principles.   *ibid.*

I hereby declare on my honour that in my whole life, whether in my youth or later, I have never read a single book of *George Sand*. Once I did begin on *Consuelo* in translation, but immediately put it down, since it seemed to me to be the product of a dilettante philosopher and not of a writer.
                    Letter, 1896

Concerning dramatic structure, I owe absolutely nothing to *Alexandre Dumas* – except that I have learned from his plays to avoid various really crude errors of which he is not so seldom guilty.   *ibid.*

As long as a nation considers it more important to build almshouses than theatres, as long as it would rather support a mission to the Zulus than an art gallery, then art cannot count on a healthy existence.   Letter, 1879

For the moment it is no use using one's weapons *for* art, but *against* the enemies of art. *ibid.*

Really, to defend kinsmen with books and brochures and open letters.
   Are there not, Mr Editor, more effective weapons?

> Letter to Cornelius Karel Elout, Editor of the
> *Algemeen Handelsblad* in Amsterdam, 1900

Since the Royal Theatre [in Copenhagen] is not willing to pay me a percentage of the box office receipts, I am compelled to find my main income by the sale of the book [*Pillars of Society*] in the shops ... Another side of the matter is that I consider it injurious for a dramatic work to be first made available to the public by a stage performance [because it] can never be understood and judged in isolation, essentially as a piece of literature. Judgement will always include both the piece and its performance ... these two completely different things are confused, and the main interest of the public is directed more towards the acting, the performance, the actors, than towards the play itself.

> Letter to Edvard Fallesen, Director of the
> Royal Theatre in Copenhagen, 1877

Captain Horst [in *An Enemy of the People*] is a *young* man; he is one of the 'young people' whom [Dr Stockman] says he likes to have in his house. The short dialogue between Horst and Petra [Dr Stockman's daughter] in the fifth act must be acted in such a way that one senses the beginning of a warm and passionate relationship between these two.

> Letter, 1882

I also take the liberty of suggesting that in the fourth act [of *An Enemy of the People*] good actors be used for the minor characters as far as possible; the more characteristic, realistic figures in the crowd, the better.

> *ibid.*

I am not particularly familiar with Byron; but I have a feeling that his works, translated into our language, would help considerably in sweeping a great deal of moral prejudice away from our artistic views, and much would thereby be achieved ... a foreign authority carries weight; and just as poetry in Germany, it is agreed, has needed Byron to attain its present level so, in my view, we need him to escape ours.

> Letter, 1872

I believe that a poem ought to be translated in the way the poet himself would have composed it, had he belonged to the nation for which he is being translated.   *ibid.*

Peer Gynt ... is considered by many people to be my best work. I have no idea to what extent it will please you. It is wild and formless, written ruthlessly, in a way I could only dare to write when far away from home. It was produced during my stay on Ischia and at Sorrento during the summer of 1867.

Letter to Edmund Gosse, 1872

It is a part of my own spiritual life that I am putting into this book [*Emperor and Galilean*]; what I describe, I have myself experienced in other forms, and the particular historical theme has a more intimate connection with the concerns of our own times than one might imagine at first sight. I regard that as imperative in any modern treatment of such distant material if, considered as literature, it is to arouse interest.   *ibid.*

You believe that my play [*Emperor and Galilean*] ought to have been written in verse ... There I must disagree with you, for you will have observed that the play has been cast in the most realistic form; the illusion I wanted to create was that of reality; I wanted to bring forth in the reader the illusion that what he read had really happened. Had I used verse, I would have thwarted my own intention ... The many everyday and insignificant characters I had deliberately put into the piece would have been obliterated and mixed up with each other if I had allowed them all to talk in a rhythmic metre ... All in all, the language must be adjusted to the degree of realism that colours the work.   Letter to Edmund Gosse, 1874

When I was writing *Brand*, I kept a scorpion in an empty beer bottle on my table. Now and then the animal was sick; then I used to throw it a piece of soft fruit, which it hurled itself on with fury and into which it poured out its poison; then it became healthy again.

Is there not something similar in us poets? The laws of Nature hold for the intellectual field as well.   Letter, 1870

Brand is myself in my best moments, just as certainly as I have presented many characteristics through self-dissection ... in Peer Gynt.   *ibid.*

The surroundings exert great influence on the forms in which the power of imagination creates.   *ibid.*

The Romance languages do not lend themselves to the
translation of … Goethe's *Faust* [with the] Gothic tone of its
language.

Letter, 1888

For my part, I do not see any disaster if the literary left wing be
shattered. I believe that these many highly talented authors are
best served by working separately without looking sideways
for a common cause.

Letter, 1883

One must have something to write about; substance within
one's life. Without that, one does not create; one only writes
books.

Letter, 1870

In an intellectual sense, mankind is after all a long-sighted
creature; we see most clearly at a great distance. The details
disturb; one has to get out of that which one wants to judge;
you depict summer best on a winter's day.

ibid.

It is not a question of wanting this or that, but wanting what
one absolutely must do, because you are yourself and can do
nothing else. Anything else simply leads to lies.

ibid.

Take no notice of other people's advice.

Letter, 1888

First and foremost [*Rosmersholm*] is naturally about human
beings and human fates.

Letter, 1887

You maintain that because of its ending the work [*A Doll's
house*] does not fall into the category of 'play'. But, honoured
herr direktor, do you really put such great store by so-called
categories? For my part, I believe that dramatic categories are
elastic, and must adjust to existing literary facts and not the
other way about.

Letter to Heinrich Laube, Director of the
Stadttheater in Vienna, 1880

Unfortunately it is not within my powers to work honestly for
the good of the working class.

Letter, 1888

The significance of the verse about which you ask is as follows: Peer Gynt invokes that fact that he has been a slave trader as justification for entering hell. To this, 'The Thin One' replies that many have done worse things, for example, to suppress the intellect, mind and will power, in their surroundings, but if such is done trivially, i.e., without demonic seriousness, they cannot even qualify for entrance into hell, but only into the 'melting ladle'.

Letter, 1880

Nothing helps a human being to mature more than to acquire thorough knowledge in one direction or another.

Letter, 1879

Without thorough historical knowledge, an author of today is at a great disadvantage, because without it, he can only judge his own times and the motives and actions of his contemporaries imperfectly and superficially.

ibid.

There is an attempt to make me responsible for the opinions expressed by some of the characters in the drama [*Ghosts*]. And yet in the whole work, there is not a single opinion, not a single line, that can be laid at the author's door. I took great care of that. The method, the kind of technique on which the form of the book is based, automatically forbade the author to be visible in the lines. My aim was to produce in the reader the impression that during his reading, he experienced a piece of reality. But nothing would have thwarted that aim to a greater degree than to insert the author's opinions into the dialogue.

Letter, 1882

It is said that [*Ghosts*] preaches nihilism. Not at all. It is not concerned with proclaiming anything at all. It only points out that under the surface, nihilism is fermenting both at home and elsewhere.

ibid.

The object is essentially to protect what is one's own, to keep it free of everything irrelevant externally, and in addition to distinguish clearly for oneself between what has seen and what one has experienced; because only the latter can be the subject of poetry.

Letter, 1870

I have myself been a theatre manager; I know that in 99 cases out of 100 the actors are incontrovertibly wrong in disputes with the management. 'Vae victis!' was the motto in olden times, and so it ought to be today … An actor works in circumstances completely different from any other artist; he is nothing in himself alone, he belongs to a complicated machine in which, in a regulated manner, he has to work. And if he has chosen the work, then he must accept the consequences the work entails. This is not hard-heartedness, but the result of bitter experience.

ibid.

Art forms die out just as the peculiar animal forms of prehistory died out, when their time had come.

Letter, 1883

The use of verse has caused the art of acting untold harm.

ibid.

Declamation is not dramatic art.

ibid.

In the past 7 – 8 years, I have scarcely written a single verse, but exclusively cultivated the incomparably more difficult art of writing purely realistic everyday language.

ibid.

To *live* – is war with the demons
That rage in heart and mind.
To *write* – is to hold
A day of judgment over yourself.

Verse written by Ibsen in the guest book of a hotel in
Gossensass, South Tyrol, 10 August 1883

The Spirit of the Times

Humanitarian! That flabby word
Is the war cry of the whole wide world!
With this each bungler hides the fact
That he dare not and he will not act.
With this each weakling masks the lie,
That he'll risk all for victory.
With this each coward dares to cloak
Vows faintly made and broken too.
In the end you dwarfish souls
A humanitarian will make of Man!

Brand, Act III, 1866

The time's humane, demands compliance,
Not blunt and absolute defiance.
Remember that this land is free;
Here all opinions will apply.
Shall *one* against the *mass* propound
His special views on black and white?
In short, you having a majority,
Are best entitled to authority.
So I submit as the others did,
And hope to suffer no reproach,
For not fighting to the last.

ibid., Act IV

Far worse times and evil visions,
Pierce the gloom of future years!
Britain's sickly cloud of coal,
Sinks in black fumes on the land,
Smothering what is fresh and green,
Strangling all the tender blooms,
Drenched with poison, sweeping low,
Stealing sunlight from the fields,
Pouring down like rain of ashes,
On the city doomed of old.

ibid., Act V

Tell me, in what year will come,
That time we call the future?

ibid.

    I think
That in each and every word of yours,
I notice signs of the ferment of the age,
For that there is ferment is clear,
Observe the reverence all refuse,
To custom hallowed by the past.   *ibid.*

That is what is so strange, Pastor Manders – there is really
nothing new in these books; there is nothing else but what
most people think and believe. It is simply that most people
don't learn about it, or won't accept it.

                                        Ghosts, Act I, 1881

Mrs Alving: Does that mean that you don't know what you
    condemn?
Pastor Manders: I have read enough *about* these publications to
    disapprove of them.
Mrs Alving: Yes, but your own opinions –
Pastor Manders: My dear lady, there are many occasions in life
    when one has to depend on others. That is the way of the
    world, and that is the way it should be. Otherwise what
    would happen to society?   *ibid.*

From our office, nothing ever goes out.

                                Love's Comedy, Act II, 1862

The old ones were bad, but the young ones are much worse!
                                        Peer Gynt, Act II, 1867

    Absolute reason
passed away last night at eleven o'clock precisely.

                                        ibid., Act IV

Fallow the missionary's field was not,
Since the Gods who were being hawked around,
Were all checkmated by the priests.   *ibid.*

Among human beings there is no more faith,
No Christianity as it's written and told.   *ibid.*, Act V

Now you understand how the zeitgeist has cast its shadow
both in my domestic life and in my professional duties. Ought I
not to oppose this corrupting, destructive and subversive
zeitgeist with all the weapons I can muster?

                                Rosmersholm, Act I, 1886

There is always some conflict or other in a family. Especially in times like ours.

ibid.

The spirit of rebellion has penetrated the school itself ... my own school [and] the most depressing aspect of the affair is that it is all the talented boys in the class who have joined together in this conspiracy against me. It is only the dullards and failures who have kept out of it.

You cannot imagine how the zeitgeist has penetrated all over the country. Almost every single concept has been turned upside down. *ibid.*

It is a storm–driven era in which we breathe. *ibid.*

Brendel: Can you spare an ideal or two?
Rosmer: What do you mean?
Brendel: A couple of discarded ideals; you will be doing a good deed. Because now I haven't any left.

ibid., Act V

In our times, the task of every piece of literature is to move the frontier posts.

Entry in a German author's autograph album, 1882

First and foremost, what I wish you is a proper, full-blooded egoism ... Don't interpret this as a sign of something brutal in my nature! You cannot benefit society in any better way than by working the metal you have in yourself. I have never really had any strong feeling for solidarity ... and if one really had the courage completely to ignore it, then perhaps one could abandon the ballast that weighs down the personality worst of all.

Letter, 1871

There are times when the whole history of the world seems to me just one long shipwreck; all that matters is to save oneself.

ibid.

Is not every generation born with contemporary assumptions? have you never noticed that in a collection of portraits from previous centuries, there is a singular family resemblance between different people of the same period? So too in the intellect.

ibid.

What will be the result of this fight to the death between two epochs, I have no idea ... I don't expect much lasting improvement ... all evolution hitherto has been vacillation from one delusion to the other.

Letter, 1872

The work I am now publishing, will be my main work. It bears the title *Emperor and Galilean* [It] deals with the conflict between two irreconcilable forces in the world, which will everlastingly be repeated ... In the character of [Caesar], as in most of what I have written in later years, there is more than I have spiritually gone through than I care to reveal in public.

Letter, 1873

Emperor and Galilean is the first work that I have written under the influence of German intellectual life ... In the autumn of 1868 I left Italy and settled down in Dresden ... Then I experienced the great times in Germany, the [Franco-Prussian war of 1870] and the consequent development. In many ways, all this exercised on me the power of transformation. My view of world history and human life had hitherto been a national view. Then it expanded to a tribal view.

Letter, 1888

The age is hungering for *beauty*.

'Balloon letter to a Swedish lady', 1870

My friend, the ship called Europe is now heading
Out to sea, bound for foreign coasts,
And tickets, you and I we now have bought,
And taken our places both upon the stern,
Waving at the old familiar strand ...
And yet, – far out upon the open sea ...
Of our happiness we seem to have been robbed ...
One night I sat alone up here on deck ...
All the passengers had by then turned in ...
But restless and uneasily they dozed ...
Here a statesman lay twisting his mouth
As if in a smile that ended in a croak ...
And someone said out loud, and as it seemed,
Suspended half way between nightmare and sickly sleep:
I think we're sailing with a corpse on board!

'A Rhymed Letter', 1875

National Characteristics

Monsieur Ballon: You are Norwegian?
Peer Gynt: By birth indeed,
But in spirit a citizen of the world.
For such fortune as I have enjoyed,
I can thank America.
My amply furnished bookshelves,
I owe to the later German schools.
From France again, I have my clothes,
My manners and my touch of wit. –
From England an industrious hand,
And self-interest nursed with heightened care.

Peer Gynt, Act IV, 1867

I would not willingly see my little son belong to a people [the
Norwegians] whose aim is to become Englishmen instead of
human beings.

Letter, 1865

More and more I feel it a painful lack in myself that I did not
learn to speak English at the right time. Now it is too late! Had
I mastered the language, I would travel over to London
immediately. Or more properly, I would have been there long
ago. I have lately been thinking a great deal, and have a
distinct feeling that my Scots ancestry has put deep marks in
me. But this is only an impression – perhaps merely a wish that
it might be so.

Letter to William Archer, 1895

There is no nation into whose literary world it would be a
greater honour for me to be introduced than the English.

Letter to Edmund Gosse, 1872

The English nation is so very closely related to us
Scandinavians; and it is precisely on that account that I find it
painful to think that language should be a barrier between my
work and the whole of this great kindred world. You may
imagine, therefore, what pleasure you gave me when you
raised the possibility of breaking down this barrier.

ibid.

How has Prussia bought the power of its state? By identifying the individual with a political and geographical concept. The waiter is the best soldier. And on the other hand, the Jewish people, mankind's aristocracy. How have they preserved themselves in isolation, in poetry, despite all the brutality from outside? Because they have no state to burden them. If they had remained in Palestine, they would have been destroyed by building it up, like all other nations.

Letter, 1871

I believe that national consciousness is in the process of dying out, and that it will be replaced by tribal consciousness. In any case I for my part have gone through that evolution. I began by feeling Norwegian, then Scandinavian, and have now ended in the broad Germanic.

Letter, 1888

You really must see Italy, not on a hasty visit, but on a long stay. Get a travel grant; don't apply, but insist, demand.

Letter, 1867

The advantage of living abroad is that one receives the national life gutted and selected.

ibid.

On Himself

You say that now I've become 'conservative'.
I'm what I have been all my life.

I do not accept just moving the pieces.
Overturn the board; there you see what I am.
                    'To my friend the Revolutionary Orator!', 1871

Only one revolution can I recall
That wasn't made by a half-baked cheat.

For all that followed, it bears the glory.
I mean of course the deluge story.

But even *then* Lucifer was cheated;
Since Noah of course the dictatorship seized.

Let's do it again, but more radical still,
But that needs men and orators too.

Now you take care of the deluge on Earth,
With pleasure I'll torpedo the Ark.

ibid.

I know that I have the failing of not coming close to those
people who want to open up completely. I have something of
the poet in The Pretenders; I can never bring myself to bare
myself completely. I have a feeling that all I have available in
personal relations is a false expression of that which I bear
deep within me, and which is really myself; therefore I prefer
to keep it locked up inside, and that is why we sometimes seem
to stand as if we were observing each other at a distance.

Letter, 1864

I have not yet been able to understand the ancient world, I
don't understand its connection with our times; I miss the
illusion, and above all the personal and individual expression
both in the artist and the work of art, and I cannot help that, so
far, I often only see custom, where others maintain that there
are laws.

ibid.

If I had to explain the chief outcome of my journey [to Italy] so far, I should say that it is that I have got rid of aestheticism, isolated, and claiming to be an end in itself, which previously had me in its grip. Aestheticism in that sense, it now seems to me, is just as great a curse for poetry, as theology for religion.

Letter, 1865

Is it not an indescribable happiness to be able to write?

ibid.

Do you know that all my life I have kept away from my own parents; from my whole family, because I cannot remain in a state of half-baked understanding?

Letter, 1867

The worst that a human being can do to himself is to do wrong to others.

ibid.

Don't think that I am some blind, vain fool! You must realise that in the silent watches of the night, I dig around, and probe and anatomise quite cheerfully in my own viscera; and what is more at those points where it hurts the most.

ibid.

I feel my powers rise with fury.   *ibid.*

I cannot deny that sometimes I feel the lack of a regular and responsible occupation.

Letter, 1884

Very likely this play [*Ghosts*] is rather daring in various respects. But I thought the time had come to move some frontier posts. And as an elder man of letters I found it easier to do that business than the many younger authors who wanted something similar.

Letter, 1882

I have never belonged, and probably never will belong to any political party whatsoever.

Letter, 1890

It has become a fundamental necessity for me to work absolutely independently and to follow my own course.

ibid.

Concerning those passages in *Peer Gynt*, I cannot agree with you. Naturally I bow to the laws of beauty; but I don't care a fig for its rules. You mention Michelangelo; but in my view, no one has sinned against the rules of beauty more than just he himself; but everything that he has created is beautiful nonetheless; since it has character.   Letter, 1869

In *Peer Gynt* I have used my own childhood circumstances and recollections.   Letter, 1882

Liberty, equality and fraternity are no longer the same as they were in the days of the blessed guillotine. That is what the politicians will not understand, and therefore I hate them. Those people only want special revolutions, revolutions of the surface, in politics, etc. But all this is nonsense. What is needed is the revolt of the human spirit.   Letter, 1870

Friends are an expensive luxury; and when one sinks all one's capital in a vocation and a mission in life, then one cannot afford to have friends. The extravagance of keeping friends lies not in what one does for them, but what, out of consideration for them, one omits to do. On that account, many intellectual shoots are crippled in oneself. I have gone through this, and on that account I have several years behind me, in which I did not succeed in being myself.   *ibid.*

Concerning the agitation against you, the lies, backbiting, etc., I will give you some advice, which I know from my own experience is absolutely sound. Be dignified! Dignity is the only weapon against such things. Always appear the same; never answer in the newspapers. If you polemicise in your writings, never direct your polemics against this or that particular attack. Never let them see that a single word of your enemies has hurt you; in a word, behave as if you have not detected any opposition. And what power do you think that your opponents' attacks have? Previously, when I read an attack on myself in the morning, I thought: now I'm finished, I can never raise myself up again! But I raised myself nonetheless; nobody remembers any more what was written, and I myself have forgotten it long ago.   Letter, 1872

It is clear to me, at any rate, that he that is alone is the strongest.
                    ibid.

I do not have the talent to be a respectable citizen.
                    Letter, 1882

To me, liberty is the first and greatest necessity of life.

ibid.

Under any circumstances, I could never join a party that had the majority behind it. *ibid.*

Where *An Enemy of the People* is concerned … I maintain that an intellectual pioneer can *never* secure a majority. In ten years, the majority has reached the standpoint of Dr. Stockmann during the meeting. But during those ten years, the doctor has not been standing still; he is still at least ten years ahead of the majority; the majority, the masses, the crowd never catch him up; he can never have the majority around him. Where I myself am concerned, in any case, I sense such an incessant advance. Where I stood when I wrote my various plays, a fairly compact crowd now stands; but I myself am no longer there; I am somewhere else, further ahead, I hope.   Letter, 1883

The explanation of my persistent silence is that more and more I lapse into dealing with one single thing at a time … Ever since my return here [Munich] I have been plagued by a new play [*Rosmersholm*] that absolutely had to emerge, and it was only at the beginning of last month that I managed to squeeze it out.

ibid., 1886

I am busy with the preparations for a great new work [*John Gabriel Borkman*] and I do not want to leave it longer than necessary. I could so easily be hit by a tile on the head before I had 'the time for the final verse'. And what then?

Letter, 1896

You are much mistaken if you believe that I want you to smash your lyre.

Letter to Theodor Caspari, contemporary
Norwegian poet, 1884

Among my other faults, I also suffer from dilatoriness in replying to letters received. *ibid.*

I well remember that I once expressed myself somewhat disrespectfully about the art of poetry; but that stemmed from my own immediate attitude to this form of art. I have long since ceased enunciating general principles, because I no longer believe that they can be established with any justification.

ibid.

All winter I have been considering new follies, and played with them to the extent that they took on dramatic form, and now I have just finished a play in five acts [*The Wild Duck*].

ibid.

I am not fighting for a troublefree existence, but for the task which I unshakeably believe and know that God has given me – that task which appears to me the most necessary and important in Norway; that is to awaken the people and make them think big.

Appeal to King Charles XV of Sweden-Norway
for an annual stipend, 1866

There is something oppressive, something depressing in the fact that people are always too late when they finally are prepared to make up for what they have neglected. Where I am concerned, I do not care at all; but I am irritated, embittered and disgusted when I notice such things happening to those that I respect and admire.

Letter, 1883

Public opinion has now settled down with respect to this serious work [*Ghosts*].

Letter, 1886

In Berchtesgaden, I had the pleasure of receiving your … review of *Peer Gynt* in the *Spectator*. I could scarcely hope for a clearer, better and more favourable interpretation of my poem. I only wish that the praise you heap upon my work was wholly deserved. The reservations you advance are undoubtedly justified; I myself can partly see the imperfections, now that after the long time that has passed, I am so far removed from the play, that I am able to look back on it as if it were the work of a stranger.

Letter to Edmund Gosse, 1872

I propose to adapt *Peer Gynt* – of which a third edition will soon appear – for performance on the stage. Will you compose the necessary music?

Letter to Edvard Grieg, 1874

It is now 40 years since we learned to know each other. Neither of us possessed many worldly goods then. In any case I did not. But in the meantime, we have done quite well, each in his own way.

You soon learned to love work. Only later did I appreciate the satisfaction of working. But on the other hand, I learned to appreciate it properly.

> Letter to Karl Hals, a Norwegian
> piano manufacturer, 1890

Everything that I have produced has its origin in a mood and an episode from life; I have never written because, as one says, I have 'found a good subject.'

> Letter, 1870

[Please] buy me a ticket ... in the Copenhagen municipal lottery; I have absolutely no hope of winning, but I like the excitement.

> Letter, 1866

It is wrong [to say] that I have studied Heine deeply ... The same applies to Kierkegaard, of whom I have read little and understood even less. – I would be interested, by the way, to know who the man is.

> Letter, 1867

Peer Gynt is a real person who lived in Gudbrundsdalen, most probably at the end of the last century or the beginning of this one. His name is still well known among the population up there, but not much more is known about his escapades than is to be found in [a Norwegian folk tale]. Thus I have not had much to base my poem on, but by the same token it has given me all the more licence.

> *ibid.*

I have heard that he [Georg Brandes] has written a dissertation on humour, a concept which, I must admit that, theoretically speaking, I am not clear over, and which I would particularly like to see resolved by Brandes in particular.

> *ibid.*

Here on Ischia ... the temperature has sometimes reached 30 degrees Reaumur [37°C], and if one is to work with a will under those conditions, one must be strong, which, thank God, I am.

> *ibid.*

I can assure you I have had a pleasant journey. I have been all the way down to [the Sudan], thereafter to the Red Sea, had many adventures and on top of all made the acquaintance of many interesting people. But best of all nonetheless is to sit quietly at home and look back on it all.

Letter, 1869

This piece [*Emperor and Galilean*] has been a Herculean task – not in the writing, because that has been easy, but the effort it has cost me to identify convincingly and graphically with such a distant and alien age. I am very pleased that your … letter holds out the prospect of good sales, because many years of my life have been devoted to this book.

Letter to Frederik Hegel, his publisher, 1873

My new work is progressing rapidly; in a few days I will have the first act ready, and for me that is always the most difficult part of a play. The title … will be *Pillars of Society*, drama in five acts. This work … will stir up a number of the more important questions of the day. For the moment, however, I must ask you to keep this between ourselves; a little later, I would very much like it to be known, since I believe that a little talk in advance among the public will help to increase the receipts.

Letter to Frederik Hegel, 1875

Naturally I will not venture on any interpretation of my own works. It would be best if the critics and the public were allowed to frolic in that field to their heart's content – until further notice, at any rate.

Letter, 1880

[*Ghosts*] has the future on its side. Those creatures who have snarled over it are not even related to their own times.

Letter, 1882

For the moment I am fully occupied with the preparations for a new play [*An Enemy of the People*]. This time it will be an uncontroversial piece, which can be read by cabinet ministers and businessmen and their ladies, and from which the theatres need not shrink.

ibid.

Herewith I have the pleasure of forwarding to you the remainder of the manuscript of my new piece [*An Enemy of the People*]. Doing this work has entertained me, and I feel a deprivation and emptiness now that I have finished with it. Dr Stockmann and I got on so well with each other; we agree on so much, but the doctor has a more confused head than I, and besides he has various other peculiarities which ensure that one is prepared to listen to a great deal from his lips, which one would not perhaps have accepted so readily if I had said it.

Letter to Frederik Hegel, 1882

It is with utter indifference that I regard the critical disturbance and all the insanity written about *Ghosts*. I was prepared for this ... There were screams about *Peer Gynt*, and not less against *Pillars of Society* and *A Doll's House*. The screams will die away on this occasion as they did previously.

Letter to Frederik Hegel, 1882

Together with this letter I send you the manuscript of my new play *The Wild Duck*, which has occupied me daily for the last four months, and parting with which is not without a certain sense of loss. Despite their manifold frailties, daily contact has nonetheless made me fond of the the people in this play.

Letter to Frederik Hegel, 1884

In certain respects [*The Wild Duck*] occupies a place of its own in my dramatic production; the construction deviates in different ways from my earlier work. However I do not wish to elaborate on this any further. Presumably the critics will find the points; in any case they will find much to argue about, much to interpret.

ibid.

I believe that *The Wild Duck* may perhaps entice some of our younger dramatists into new paths, and that I consider to be desirable.

ibid.

The sight of the sea is what I miss most out here [Rome], and that longing increases year by year.

Letter, 1885

My sketches possess scarcely any artistic value. If they are reproduced, it must really be as curiosities.

Letter, 1886

I am travelling to Berlin ... where *Ghosts* is to be produced at
the Residentz Theatre. I would rather have stayed at home, but
after the many invitations I have received, I cannot easily
decline to be present, especially since *Ghosts* has become a
burning literary and dramatic issue in Germany.
In Berlin, I am prepared for considerable opposition from the
conservative press. But for me that is also a contributory reason
to be present.

Letter, 1887

In Meiningen, the Duke gave me an almost demonstrative
distinction in that the day after the performance [of *Ghosts*] – to
quote the diploma 'as a token of his respect and honour' – he
decorated me with the insignia of the Saxon Ernestine Order as
a Commander, First Class, with star.

You must not imagine that I mention this out of vanity. But I
cannot deny that it pleases me, when I think back on the stupid
denunciation to which the play was subjected for a long time at
home.

ibid.

I almost never go to the theatre ... but now and then I like to
read a play in the evening, and since I have a powerful
imagination where the drama is concerned ... reading almost
has the effect of a stage production.

Letter, 1888

Brand is a work of art and not an iota more. What it might have
built up or broken down is absolutely no concern of mine. It
was at the time the result of something experienced – not lived
through. It was necessary for me to liberate myself through the
medium of poetry from something within myself with which I
was finished; and when by this means I was free of it, my play
no longer had any interest for me.

Letter, 1870

You mustn't think that I am so hostile to my compatriots as
many accuse me of being. And in any case, I can assure you
that I am not friendlier to myself than to others.

ibid.

During ten years of literary activity, and even during a longer period of preparation that preceded it, a concern with the principles, system and history of dramatic art and literature has occupied most of my time and been my essential study. The reviews of my dramatic works which have been published during this period both by foreign and domestic critics, presumably contains sufficient evidence that this study has not been without result.

> Application to the Norwegian Government
> for a travel grant, 1860

In this country, to live exclusively, or even mainly on literary activity, is an impossibility. [To] renounce an activity which I have hitherto considered, and still consider my real life's work is, however, a step which I would find unspeakably harsh, and it is in order, if possible, to avoid this, that I now make my last attempt, that is to say I most humbly request that a proposal be put before the assembled Parliament that I be awarded an annual stipend out of the State budget ... so that I may be put into a position to continue my work in the service of literature which, I have reason to believe, the public do not wish to be discontinued.

> Application to the Norwegian Government for
> an annual stipend, 1863

For my part, I need another year's stay here [in Rome], if my journey is not to be more than half destroyed. In addition, I am preparing an extensive dramatic work, the material for which is taken from Roman history. This work, which I have begun here, I must finish here; to change residence in the middle of such a task is the same as changing mood and intellectual point of view; something from which the unity of the work would at least suffer, if not be completely destroyed.

> Application for a travel grant to the Norwegian
> Society for the Arts and Sciences, 1865

Of all my works, I consider *Peer Gynt* the least likely to be understood outside the Scandinavian countries.

> Letter, 1880

Everything that I have written is closely related to something that I have lived through.

> *ibid.*

Peer Gynt is absolutely not intended to be performed.

> Letter, 1881

[After finishing *Hedda Gabler*] It is just as well that it came to an end. The endless cohabitation with these imaginary people had begun to make me not a little nervous.

Letter, 1890

The name of the play is Hedda Gabler. In this way [using her maiden name] I wanted to indicate that where her personality is concerned, she is to be considered more as her father's daughter than her husband's wife.
  In this play I did not want to deal with so-called problems. For, the main thing has been to depict human beings, human moods and human fates, on the basis of certain reigning social conditions and opinions.   *ibid*

I am responsible for what I write, I and no one else … I want to be like a lonely *franc-tireur* among the outposts and operating on his own.   Letter, 1882

To the eyes of an outsider, it might seem that I have deliberately made myself a stranger to my family … but I dare to say that from the beginning, inexorable circumstances have played the greatest part.

Letter to Christian Paus, his uncle, 1877

From my 14th year I have been thrown on my own resources; for many years I have had to fight hard to plough my furrow and attain the point where I now stand. The main reason that I so seldom wrote home during all these years of struggle is that I was in no position to support my parents; I thought it was useless to write when I was unable to act; I always hoped that my circumstances would improve, but that happened very late, and not long ago.   *ibid.*

I look into myself; that is where I have my battleground, where sometimes I conquer, and sometimes suffer defeat.

Letter, 1869

I have always been fond of stormy weather.

Letter, 1891

If ever I accomplish a great work,
It will be a deed of darkness.   'Fear of the Light', 1871

I prefer to ask; to answer is not my concern.

'A Rhymed Letter', 1875

On his Compatriots

We are not used to resonance,
For in this land, it is so rare.   *Brand*, Act V, 1866

A middling town, offering no pleasure, but only entertainment.
                                                  Ghosts, Act II, 1881

The cow gives cake and mead, the bull;
Ask not if it is sweet or sour,
The main point is, and don't forget,
In this country, it is all made.   *Peer Gynt*, Act II, 1867

They can agree on one thing alone,
That every great man must be toppled and stoned.
                                           The Pretenders, Act V, 1864

If I were to return home now, one of two things would happen:
either I would make enemies out of everyone at home, or I
would once more slip into all kinds of disguises and become a
lie both to myself and to others.

                                                      Letter, 1867

Go abroad, carissimo! Both because distance gives a broader
vision, and because at the same time the hoi polloi are out of
sight. I am quite sure that at the time the inhabitants of Weimar
were Goethe's worst audience.

                                                            ibid.

No, the fact is that I would not be able to write freely and
uninhibitedly and frankly [in Norway].

                                                      Letter, 1884

Ten years ago, after my second absence of ten years, when I
sailed up the fjord, I literally felt my chest contract with
revulsion and a feeling of sickness. I felt the same during my
whole stay up there; I was no longer myself among all these
cold and uncomprehending Norwegian eyes in the windows
and on the pavements.   *ibid.*

At home one thinks and feels locally, not nationally.
                                                      Letter, 1875

In Norway, I do believe that in most cases the fuss [about *Ghosts*] has been involuntary; and that has an obvious explanation. Up there, you see, criticism is partially exercised by some more or less disguised theologians, and those gentlemen are as a rule completely incapable of writing sensibly about works of literature. Letter, 1882

At home there is not much interest in freedom, but only in freedoms, a few more or a few less, according to party views.
ibid.

During the highly laudable efforts to turn our people into a democratic society, we have inadvertently gone far to make ours a plebeian society. *ibid.*

Your fellow-countrymen are now proud of you nonetheless, even if they cannot forbear to attack you now and then. I am familiar with attitudes of that kind.

Letter to Georg Brandes, 1883

I would find it impossible to settle down permanently in Norway. Nowhere else do I feel more homeless than up there. The old concept of a fatherland is no longer enough for a reasonably intellectually developed human being.

Letter, 1888

Up here among the fjords I have my native land. But-but-but: where do I find my homeland? Letter, 1896

It would be most desirable for your future literary activity that you should quickly have the opportunity personally to make yourself acquainted with broader and untrammelled fields of contemporary life than those to which you have hitherto been confined … I know what I owe to my knowledge of the world outside, and I often think with sympathy of the many gifted people at home who are hampered by narrow horizons.

Letter to Kristian Elster, contemporary
Norwegian author, 1880

In Norway, I understand, [*Peer Gynt*] has caused a great fuss; that worries me not in the least; but both there and [elsewhere] people have found more satire than I intended. Why can't they read the book as a poem? Because that is how I have written it. The satirical passages are fairly isolated. But if the present day Norwegians, as it seems, recognize themselves in the person of Peer Gynt, then that is their affair. Letter, 1868

I know the politicking ranters up there in Norway so well, and I know that they will never rise to serious action.

Letter, 1882

I fear that in the long run I would not be happy in Norway or be able to work there. The circumstances under which I work here [in Munich] are far more favourable; it is the big world with intellectual freedom and a broad view of things.

Letter, 1877

Norway is a free country inhabited by unfree people.

Letter, 1882

In Norway, how often does one not hear worthy citizens expatiate with such profound smugness on Norwegian moderation which, when all is said and done, means nothing more than that tepid average temperature of the blood which makes it impossible for proper people to commit a folly in grand style.

Letter, 1865

After returning here [Dresden], we have led a more sociable life than usual, since the place has been visited by a mass of Scandinavians ... as far as the visiting Norwegians are concerned, I assume they are driven by curiosity. I cannot count on any genuine sympathy from up there.

Letter, 1872

My countrymen, who gave me the exile's staff,
The baggage of sorrow, the swift heels of angst.

'The Millennium Jubilee', 1872

Society & the Individual

Each ordered mode of life proclaims,
One law that goes by many names.
In art it is dubbed a school,
And in the army, as I know
It is called to keep in step.
Ay yes, my friend, that's the word!
That is what the State desires.
At the double is too fast,
Marking time is much too slow –
To each a pace of equal length,
To each the same rhythm of the foot –
That's the method's final aim!   *Brand*, Act III, 1866

But if to allegory we must resort,
We'll turn to Scripture if you please.
It has evidence for every case.
From Genesis to Revelation
It swarms with stimulating fable.
I will merely point in illustration
At that projected Tower of Babel.
How far did all those people come?
And why? The answer's clear as day.
They did not keep within the ranks,
Each one his own language spoke,
They drew not in the common yoke –
In short, personalities they became.   *ibid.*

The ignorant crowd can never accept the unusual.
                    Emperor and Galilean, Part II, Act I, 1873

Helmer: You are talking like a child. You don't understand the
    society you are living in.
Nora: No I don't. But now I'm going to find out. I must
    discover who is right, society or myself.
Helmer: Now you're sick, Nora. You're feverish. I almost think
    you have taken leave of your senses.
                    A Doll's House, Act III, 1879

I can't concern myself so much with others; I'm busy enough
thinking about myself.   *Ghosts*, Act II, 1881

Mrs Stockmann: But why is every single one of them against
you, to the last man?
Dr Stockmann: I'll tell you why. It's because in this town all
men are little women – just like you; they all think only
about the family, and not about society.

An Enemy of the People, Act IV, 1882

von Eberkopf: But what is Peer Gynt himself?
Peer Gynt: The world behind my forehead's vault,
Which decides that I am no one else,
Than I, no more than God is Satan.

Peer Gynt, Act IV, 1867

Gynt himself, it is the horde,
Of wishes, appetites, desires,
Gynt himself, it is the sea
Of fancies, pretensions and demands,
In short what makes just *my* breast heave,
And whereby I exist in the way I do.   *ibid.*

Peer Gynt: Do you know what it is to live?
Anitra: Teach me!
Peer Gynt: It is to hover
Dry-shod down the river of time,
Absolutely as yourself.   *ibid.*

A bad citizen he was and profitless
For state and church. But up here on the heath,
On his family's narrow bounds, where he worked,
There he was great, because there he was himself.

ibid., Act V

Do you know what we are; we who are called pillars of
society? We are the tools of society; neither more nor less.

Pillars of Society, Act IV, 1877

The crowd is well drilled; that cannot be denied; it has a
uniformity which in some ways is exemplary. Everybody
keeps in step.   Letter, 1865

The state is the curse of the individual.   Letter, 1871

I have a horror of the crowd.

'Balloon letter to a Swedish lady', 1870

The Power of the Past

Ah, I understand; old memories are making you frightened.
A Doll's House, Act II, 1879

It is not only what we inherit from our mothers and fathers
that are repeated in us. There are all kinds of dead old opinions
and a variety of dead old beliefs and things like that. They are
not alive in us, but they are there just the same, and we cannot
get rid of them.   *Ghosts*, Act II, 1881

I am afraid and cautious, because there remains within me
something ghost-like that I can never really get rid of.

ibid.

Løvborg: This [book] is about the future.
Tesman: The future! But good heavens, we know absolutely
nothing about that.   *Hedda Gabler*, Act II, 1890

Now I put on my old clothing for the fight,
Against all modern knowledge, to tradition true!
Love's Comedy, Act II, 1862

Like a feather I'll swim on history's stream,
Live through it again, as if in a dream,
Watch heroes struggle for what is great and good,
But as a spectator only, safe and sound –
Watch ideas collapse and martyrs bleed,
Watch empires founded, and empires fall,
From small things, see the epochs grow.
In short, from history I'll skim the cream.

Peer Gynt, Act IV, 1867

The internal mechanics of history [are] cunning.   *ibid.*

The political conditions at home have saddened me greatly,
and destroyed many a pleasure for me. It has all been lies and
dreams … We can now draw a line under our ancient history;
for the modern Norwegians have obviously no more in
common with their past, than the piratical Greeks with that
breed that sailed to Troy and was helped by the Gods.

Letter, 1864

Youth & Age

There are so many untruths both in the home and at school. At home, one has to be silent, and at school we have to stand up and lie to the children.

An Enemy of the People, Act I, 1882

Is it not glorious to see young people eat? Always an appetite! And that's as it should be. Food is needed! And strength! These are the people who will stir up the fermenting material of the future.

ibid.

Now I see! Halvard Solness must begin to retire now! Give way to those who are younger! For the very youngest, perhaps! Only give way! Give way! Give way!

The Master Builder, Act I, 1892

But I will never retire! I will never give way to anyone!

ibid.

Solness: I am afraid, horribly afraid. For some time the change must come, you see.
Dr Herdal: Nonsense! Where is the change coming from?
Solness: It is coming from youth.
Dr Herdal: Nonsense! Youth? But you aren't behind the times, I am certain. You're surely just as safe in the saddle as you have ever been.
Solness: The change is coming. I sense it. And I feel that it is coming closer. Someone or other starts demanding: give way for *me!* And then all the others follow in a storm, shrieking and threatening: Give way! Give way! Give way! Just you look out, Doctor. Some time youth will come here knocking on the door.
Dr Herdal: Well, good Heavens, and what then?
Solness: What then? Why, then it is the end of the Master Builder.

ibid.

Solness: I tell you – I have begun to be so frightened of younger people, so horribly afraid.

Hilde: Rubbish – as if youth were anything to be afraid of!

Solness: But it is. That is why I have locked myself in. You must know that youth wants to come here and batter on the door! Break in to me!

Hilde: Then I think you ought to go out and let youth in.

Solness: Open up?

Hilde: Yes, so that youth can get into you. With all the good it brings.

Solness: No, no, no! Youth – No, you see, that's retribution. It comes in the vanguard of change.

ibid.

Consul Bernick: I will collapse with the whole of this bungling society. But there is a generation growing up after us; it is my son I am working for; it is for *him* that I am putting my life's work in order [and] he will build a happier existence than his father's.

Miss Hessel: With a lie as foundation? Think what you are bequeathing to your son.

Pillars of Society, Act IV, 1877